MW00803145

BEST
IN CLASS

Dear Student,

Welcome to BEST IN CLASS!

Music is an important part of our daily lives. The study of music helps us gain an appreciation for beauty and a feeling of sensitivity. It also provides an avenue for creativity and recognition, as well as a demand for self-discipline. All of these are important in our world today.

Playing a musical instrument can also give you years of enjoyment. To play your instrument well, careful practice is essential. You will find a chart below to help you keep track of your practice time. Always strive to do your best.

Best wishes in reaching your musical goals!

Bruce Pearson

PRACTICE RECORD CHART

WEEK	DAY 1	DAY 2	DAY 3	DAY 4	DAY 5	DAY 6	DAY 7	TOTAL TIME	PARENT'S INITIALS	WEEKLY GRADE
1										
2										
3										
4										
5										
6										
7										
8										
9										
10										
11										
12										
13										
14										
15										
16										
17										
18										

WEEK	DAY 1	DAY 2	DAY 3	DAY 4	DAY 5	DAY 6	DAY 7	TOTAL TIME	PARENT'S INITIALS	WEEKLY GRADE
19										
20										
21										
22										
23										
24										
25										
26										
27										
28										
29										
30										
31										
32										
33										
34										
35										
36										

© 1982 Kjos West, Publisher, San Diego, California
N   0-8497-5849-1   All Rights Reserved   International Copyright Secured   Printed in U.S.A.   W3PR

BEFORE YOU START...

SETTING UP THE SNARE DRUM

There are two generally accepted ways of holding your drum sticks. One is the TRADITIONAL GRIP and the other is the MATCHED HAND GRIP. Ask your director which he or she prefers. The grip that you use will determine how you set up your drum.

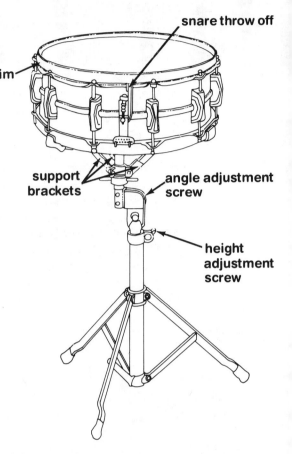

- **Matched Grip Drum Set Up**
    1) Set up your stand. The drum **support brackets** are designed so that two of them are closer together.
    2) Place the two support brackets that are closer together near you. Place the single support bracket away from you about 2 inches higher than the other two.
    3) Tighten the **angle adjustment screw.**
    4) Set your drum on the stand so that the **"snare throw off"** is toward you.
    5) Adjust the single support bracket so that it holds your drum firmly.
    6) Adjust the height of your drum so the **rim** closest to you is about 4 inches below your waist.
    7) Tighten the **height adjustment screw.**

- **Traditional Grip Drum Set Up**
    1) Set up your stand. The drum **support brackets** are designed so that two of them are closer together.
    2) Place the two support brackets that are closer together on your right. Place the single support bracket on your left about 2 inches higher than the other two.
    3) Tighten the **angle adjustment screw.**
    4) Set your drum on the stand so that the **"snare throw off"** is toward you.
    5) Adjust the single support bracket so that it holds your drum firmly.
    6) Adjust the height of your drum so the **rim** closest to you is about 4 inches below your waist.
    7) Tighten the **height adjustment screw.**

GETTING A GOOD HAND POSITION

Ask your director what grip to use.
- **The Matched Grip**
    1) Open your hand with the palm facing up.
    2) Place the drum stick diagonally across your open hand from the base of the little finger across your palm to the first joint of the index finger.
    3) Rest your thumb on the drum stick shaft where it crosses the index finger. This should be approximately one-third of the length in from the butt end. Your thumb should point toward the drum stick tip.
    4) Close your fingers gently around the drum stick shaft.
    5) Turn your hand over so that the back of your hand is up.
    6) Grip the other stick in the same way with the other hand. This is the reason it is called the "matched grip."

for drums only

- **The Traditional Grip**
  LEFT HAND:
  1) Locate an imaginary spot on the stick approximately one-third of the length in from the butt end.
  2) Rest that spot on the stick between the middle and ring fingers at the first knuckle.
  3) Rest the butt end of the stick in the web between the thumb and index finger.
  4) Curve, comfortably, your ring and little fingers under the stick and your index and middle fingers on top of the stick.
  RIGHT HAND:
  1) Open your hand with the palm facing up.
  2) Place the drum stick diagonally across your open hand from the base of the little finger across your palm to the first joint of the index finger.
  3) Rest your thumb on the drum stick shaft where it crosses the index finger. This should be approximately one-third of the length in from the butt end. Your thumb should point toward the drum stick tip.
  4) Close your fingers gently around the drum stick shaft.
  5) Turn your hand over so that the back of your hand is up.

STANDING POSITION

- Stand in a comfortable position with your feet spaced slightly apart and one foot slightly ahead of the other.
- Distribute the weight evenly on both feet.
- Stand about 12 inches from the drum.

LEARNING THE STROKE

- Strike the drum in an imaginary circle about 4 inches in diameter. This circle should be about a third of the way in from the rim and directly over the snare.
- Strike the drum with a quick snap of the wrist. Only the wrists are involved in this action. Use no arm movement.
- Imagine you are pulling the tone out of the drum. Never allow the sticks to dampen the tone.

STARTING EXERCISES

- **"One Stick Game"**
  With your right hand strike the drum 4 times with a steady rhythm, rest for 4 beats. Repeat this four times.
- **"Alternate Action"**
  With your right hand strike the drum 4 times with a steady rhythm; rest for 4 beats. With your left hand strike the drum 4 times with a steady rhythm; rest for 4 beats. Repeat this four times.

CARING FOR YOUR INSTRUMENT...

- Clean the drum heads regularly with a damp cloth.
- Never pull, pluck, or strum the snares.
- Never store any loose equipment or books in your drum case.

BEFORE YOU START...

KEYBOARD

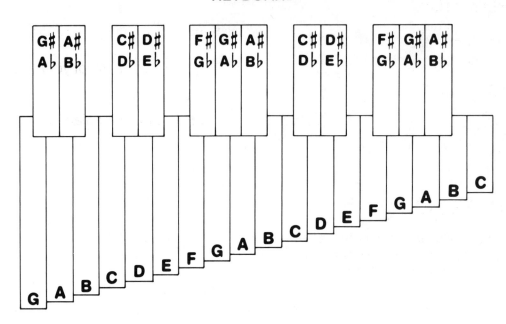

LEARNING YOUR INSTRUMENT'S RANGE

- **MARIMBA**

- **XYLOPHONE**

- **BELLS**

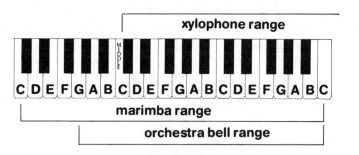

GRIPPING MALLETS

- Open your hand with the palm facing up.
- Place the mallet diagonally across your open hand from the base of the little finger across your palm to the first joint of the index finger.
- Rest your thumb on the mallet shaft where it crosses the index finger. This should be approximately one-third of the distance from the grip end of the mallet. Your thumb should point toward the head of the mallet.
- Close your fingers gently around the mallet shaft.
- Roll your hand over so that the back of your hand is up.
- Grip your mallet in the same way with the other hand.

for mallets only

STANDING POSITION

- Stand about 6 to 10 inches away from your instrument so you can easily reach the center of each bar.
- Position your feet on the floor so you are comfortably facing the middle of your instrument.
- Avoid crossing your feet while playing.
- Position the music stand as low as possible to keep from losing your balance when looking from music to keyboard.

LEARNING THE STROKE

- Hold the mallet about 2 to 3 inches above the bar.
- Strike the bar with a quick down-up snap of your wrist.
- Strike the bar in the center.
- When playing two notes in a row on one bar, keep the left mallet in front of the right.
- Maintain equal force of the stroke from each hand.

STARTING EXERCISES

- **"One Mallet Game"**
  With your director's assistance locate middle C on your instrument. With your right mallet strike middle C 4 times with a steady rhythm, rest for 4 beats. Repeat this 4 times.
- **"Alternate Action"**
  Locate middle C on your instrument. With your right mallet strike middle C 4 times with a steady rhythm, rest for 4 beats. With your left mallet strike middle C 4 times, rest for 4 beats. Repeat this exercise 4 times.

CARING FOR YOUR INSTRUMENT...

- Cover your mallet instrument when not in use.
- Never allow objects to be placed on the bars.
- Check to see that the bars are not binding against the guideposts.
- Never use metal or hard plastic mallets on wooden bars.

GETTING A HEAD START...

THE BASICS

STICKING	STAFF	MEASURES
R = right hand stick L = left hand stick		bar lines measures

THE "NATURAL" WAY TO START

STANDING	SETTING UP YOUR DRUM	HOLDING YOUR STICKS
Be sure you are standing with your feet comfortably apart, spine straight, weight balanced equally on each foot.	Check again for the correct way to set up your drum (see page 2-A).	Check again for the correct way to hold your sticks (see page 2-A).

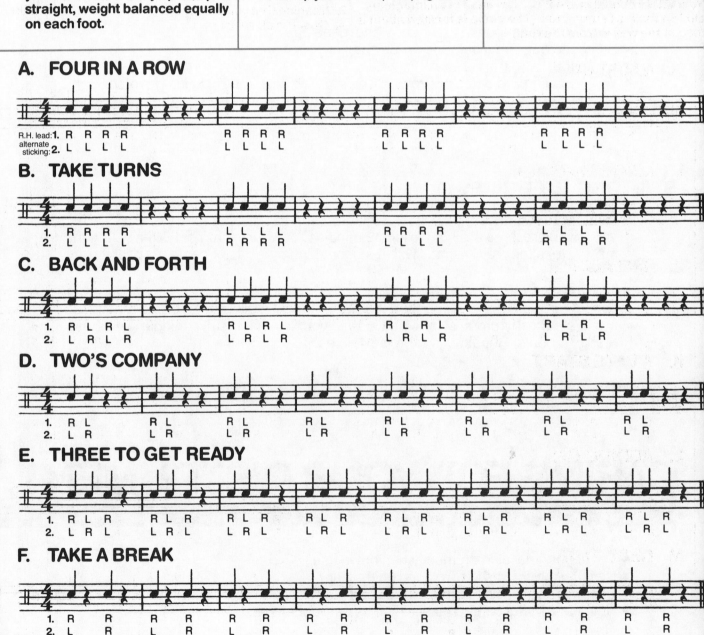

A. FOUR IN A ROW

R.H. lead: **1.** R R R R   R R R R   R R R R   R R R R
alternate sticking: **2.** L L L L   L L L L   L L L L   L L L L

B. TAKE TURNS

1. R R R R   L L L L   R R R R   L L L L
2. L L L L   R R R R   L L L L   R R R R

C. BACK AND FORTH

1. R L R L   R L R L   R L R L   R L R L
2. L R L R   L R L R   L R L R   L R L R

D. TWO'S COMPANY

1. R L   R L   R L   R L   R L   R L   R L   R L
2. L R   L R   L R   L R   L R   L R   L R   L R

E. THREE TO GET READY

1. R L R   R L R   R L R   R L R   R L R   R L R   R L R   R L R
2. L R L   L R L   L R L   L R L   L R L   L R L   L R L   L R L

F. TAKE A BREAK

1. R   R   R   R   R   R   R   R
2. L   R   L   R   L   R   L   R

G. THE OTHER WAY

1. L   L   L   L   L   L   L   L
2. R   L   R   L   R   L   R   L

for drums only

TIME SIGNATURE	QUARTER NOTE	QUARTER REST
$\frac{4}{4}$ = 4 beats in each measure	♩ = 1 beat	𝄽 = 1 beat of silence

STRIKING THE DRUM

Ask your director which sticking system to use.

Your sticks should strike the drum head in an imaginary circle 4 inches in diameter. (The circle is located about a *third* of the way in from the rim.)

MAKING THE STROKE

1. Make the stroke with a quick snap of your wrist.
2. Never allow the sticks to "dampen" the tone.
3. Imagine that you are "pulling" the tone out of the drum
4. Observe all sticking.

H. MIXED UP

I. MORE MIXED UP

J. TAG ALONG

K. A LATE START

L. ADDING ON

M. REST TIME

N. PUTTING IT TOGETHER

GETTING A HEAD START...

THE BASICS

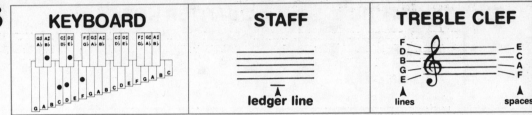

KEYBOARD | **STAFF** | **TREBLE CLEF**

ledger line

lines | spaces

THE "NATURAL" WAY TO START

★ Locate the first five notes by the dots on the keyboard above.

A. THE 1ST NOTE

B flat

NEW NOTE

B. THE 2ND NOTE

C

NEW NOTE

C. TWO'S COMPANY

D. A LITTLE EXTRA PRACTICE

E. THE 3RD NOTE

D

NEW NOTE

F. THREE TO GET READY

G. THREE STEPS

H. COMING BACK HOME

I. THE 4TH NOTE

E flat

NEW NOTE

for mallets only

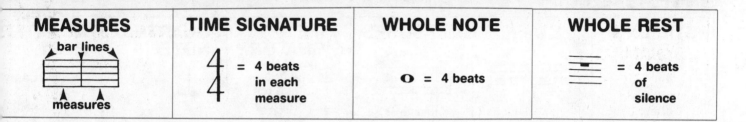

MEASURES	TIME SIGNATURE	WHOLE NOTE	WHOLE REST
bar lines / measures	4/4 = 4 beats in each measure	O = 4 beats	= 4 beats of silence

GRIPPING THE MALLETS
Check again for the correct way to grip your mallets (see page 2-B).

STRIKING THE BARS
Your mallet should strike the center of the bar.
R=right hand mallet
L=left hand mallet

MAKING THE STROKE
Make the stroke with a quick "down-up" snap of your wrist. Maintain equal force of the stroke with each hand.

STARTING TOGETHER...

THE BASICS

STICKING	STAFF	MEASURES	TIME SIGNATURE	QUARTER NOTE	QUARTER REST
R = right hand stick L = left hand stick		bar lines ... measures	$\frac{4}{4}$ = 4 beats in each measure	♩ = 1 beat	𝄽 = 1 beat of silence

1. THE 1ST NOTE / 2. THE 2ND NOTE

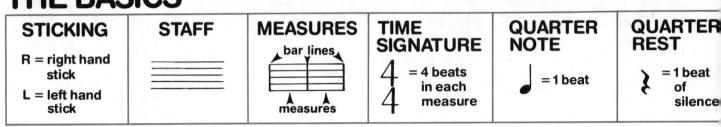

★ Ask your director which sticking system to use. Play with a steady speed (tempo).

3. WHAT A PAIR! / 4. HOW DO YOU SOUND?

★ Write in the counting for the snare drum part on the blank lines. (Your director will tell you the counting system to use.)

5. THE 3RD NOTE / 6. TWO'S COMPANY

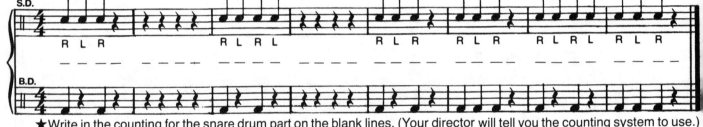

7. THREE TO GET READY / 8. A LITTLE EXTRA PRACTICE

★ Are you playing with a good hand position?

9. NAME GAME

★ Do the NAME GAME on mallet page 6-B.

THEORY GAME

for the full band

STRIKING THE DRUM		MAKING THE STROKE	
SNARE DRUM	**BASS DRUM**	**SNARE DRUM**	**BASS DRUM**
our sticks should strike e drum head in an maginary circle 4 inches diameter. (The circle is cated about a *third* of the ay in from the rim.)	Your mallet should strike the head in an area located about a *fourth* of the way in from the rim.	1. Make the stroke with a quick snap of the wrist. 2. Never allow the sticks to "dampen" the tone. 3. Imagine that you are "pulling" the tone out of the drum. 4. Observe all sticking.	1. Hold the mallet in your right hand. (The grip is the same as the right hand snare grip. See page 2-A). 2. Make the stroke with a quick snap of the wrist.

10. TWO AT A TIME / 11. THE 4TH NOTE

12. THERE'S ALWAYS ROOM FOR MORE / 13. THE 5TH NOTE

14. TWO-TIMERS / 15. FIVE MAKES A TEAM

16. FOUR IN A ROW / 17. MOVING DOWN

★Write in the counting for both parts before you play.

SOMETHING SPECIAL . . . for drums only

W3PR - Drums

STARTING TOGETHER...

THE BASICS

KEYBOARD	STRIKING THE BARS	MAKING THE STROKE	STAFF
	Your mallet should strike the center of the bar. R=right hand mallet L=left hand mallet	Make the stroke with a quick "down-up" snap of your wrist. Maintain equal force of the stroke with each hand.	 ledger line

NEW NOTE

1. THE 1ST NOTE

Play 4 times.

★ Locate the first five notes by the dots on the keyboard above.

NEW NOTE

2. THE 2ND NOTE

E flat   Play 4 times.

3. WHAT A PAIR!

★ Write in the counting on the blank lines. (Your director will tell you the counting system to use.)

4. HOW DO YOU SOUND?

⌐Band⌐ ⌐Brass⌐ ⌐Band⌐ ⌐Woodwinds⌐ ⌐Band⌐ ⌐Percussion⌐ ⌐Band⌐

★ Which section can play with the best tone quality?

NEW NOTE

5. THE 3RD NOTE

D   Play 4 times.

6. TWO'S COMPANY

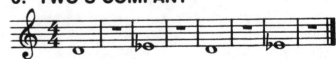

7. THREE TO GET READY

★ Are you playing with a good hand position?

8. A LITTLE EXTRA PRACTICE

THEORY GAME

9. NAME GAME

1. Write the names of the lines in the squares.

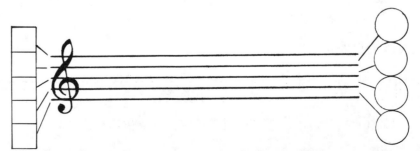

2. Write the names of the spaces in the circles.

for the full band

TREBLE CLEF	MEASURES	TIME SIGNATURE	WHOLE NOTE	WHOLE REST
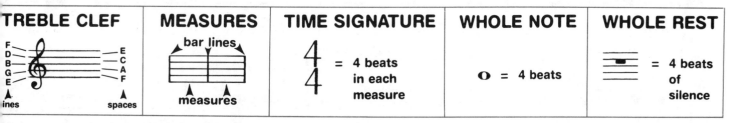 lines / spaces	bar lines / measures	4/4 = 4 beats in each measure	O = 4 beats	= 4 beats of silence

10. TWO AT A TIME

11. THE 4TH NOTE
C — Play 4 times.
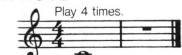

12. THERE'S ALWAYS ROOM FOR MORE

13. THE 5TH NOTE
B flat — Play 4 times.

14. TWO-TIMERS

15. FIVE MAKES A TEAM

★ Write in the note names before you play.

QUARTER NOTE	♩ = 1 beat	4/4 ...
QUARTER REST	𝄽 = 1 beat of silence	

16. FOUR IN A ROW

★ Write in the counting before you play.

17. MOVING DOWN

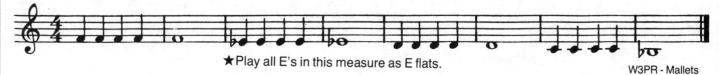

★Play all E's in this measure as E flats.

W3PR - Mallets

NEW IDEA

FERMATA (sometimes called a "hold")		Play the note until your director signals you to stop.

18. WARM-UP

A.   B. Play 2 times.

1. R L R L   R   R   R L R L   R L R   R L R L   R   R   R L R L   R   R
2. L R L R   L   R   L R L R   L R L   R L R L   R   L   R L R L   R   L

19. HOW DO YOU SOUND? / 20. IN CONCERT (Duet)

S.D.

1. R   R   R L R L   R   L R   R L R L   R   R   R L R
2. R   L   R L R L   R   L R   R L R L   R   L   R L R

★Remember . . . rests are silent beats!

B.D.

NEW IDEAS

HALF NOTE	♩ = 2 beats	
HALF REST	▬ = 2 beats of silence	

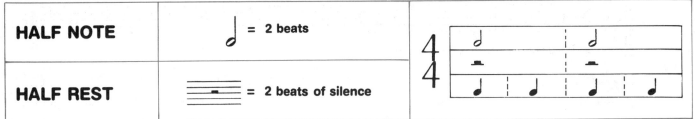

21. HALF NOTE HAPPENING / 22. MAKING MUFFINS

S.D.

B.D.

★Write in the counting before you play.

23. LITTLE ROBIN RED BREAST / 24. MERRILY WE ROLL ALONG

NEW IDEA

FLAM	RIGHT HAND FLAM  L R The left stick strikes just before the right, as if saying "f ' LAM."	LEFT HAND FLAM R L The right stick strikes just before the left, as if saying "f ' LAM."

SOMETHING SPECIAL . . . for drums only

A.

L R   L R   L R   L R   L R   L R   L R   L R

★Hold your right stick slightly higher than the left. Bring both sticks down at the same speed, allowing the left stick to strike just before the right.

B.

R L   R L   R L   R L   R L   R L   R L   R L

★Hold your left stick slightly higher than the right. Bring both sticks down at the same speed, allowing the right stick to strike just before the left.

SPECIAL EXERCISES

NEW IDEA

| FERMATA
(sometimes called a "hold") | ⌢ | Play the note until your director signals you to stop. |

18. WARM-UP

A.

B. Play 2 times.

19. HOW DO YOU SOUND?

⌊ Band ⌋ ⌊ Woodwinds ⌋ ⌊ Band ⌋ ⌊ Brass ⌋ ⌊ Band ⌋

★ Which section sounds the best?

20. IN CONCERT

A.   Duet

★ Remember . . . rests are silent beats!

B.

NEW IDEAS

| HALF NOTE | ♩ = 2 beats |
| HALF REST | ▬ = 2 beats of silence |

21. HALF NOTE HAPPENING

★ Write in the counting before you play.

22. MAKING MUFFINS

English Traditional Song

★ Do you recognize this melody?

23. LITTLE ROBIN RED BREAST

Traditional

R L R L   R L   R L R L   R   R   L R   L R   L R L R   L

★ Are you striking the bar in the proper place?

24. MERRILY WE ROLL ALONG

Traditional

★ Write in the note names before you play.

25. WARM-UP

| REPEAT SIGN |  | Play the previous section of music again. |

26. PLAYING MORE HALF NOTES AND RESTS / 27. O COME, LITTLE CHILDREN

Play 4 times.

★Write in the counting for both parts before you play.

28. START TODAY / 29. FOLLOW THAT MAN (Duet)

Play 4 times.

30. FRENCH SONG

Play 4 times.

31. SPELLING GAME

★Do the SPELLING GAME on mallet page 9-B.

| FLAM TAP |  |

SOMETHING SPECIAL . . . for drums only

A.

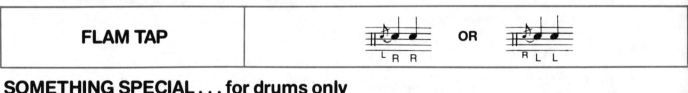

B.

25. WARM-UP

A. ⌢   B. Play 2 times.

NEW IDEA

| REPEAT SIGN | 𝄇 | Play the previous section of music again. |

26. PLAYING MORE HALF NOTES AND RESTS

27. O COME, LITTLE CHILDREN

J.A.P. Schultz

★ Write in the counting before you play.

28. START TODAY

Traditional

29. FOLLOW THAT MAN

Root - Duet

A.

B.

30. FRENCH SONG

French Folk Song

31. SPELLING GAME

THEORY GAME

P R ___ ___ T I ___ ___   M ___ K ___ S   P ___ R ___ ___ ___ T!

★ Write in the note names.

SOMETHING SPECIAL . . . for mallets only

SPECIAL EXERCISE

L R L R   L R L   L R L R   L R L   L R L R   L R L   R L R L   R

32. WARM-UP

Play 4 times.

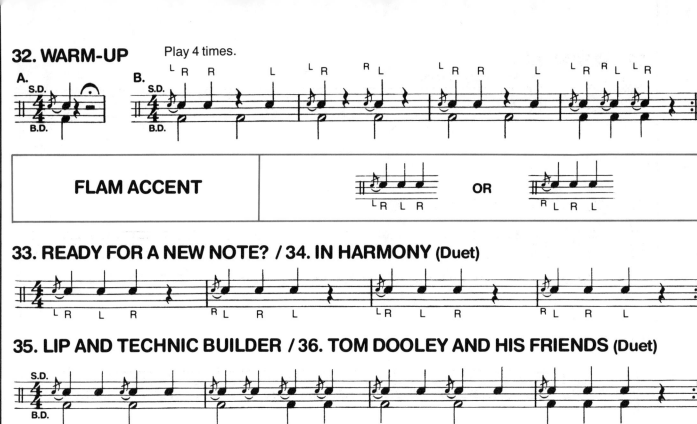

FLAM ACCENT	

33. READY FOR A NEW NOTE? / 34. IN HARMONY (Duet)

35. LIP AND TECHNIC BUILDER / 36. TOM DOOLEY AND HIS FRIENDS (Duet)

★Write in the counting for the snare drum part before you play.

37. ODE TO JOY

★Are you playing with a good hand position?

SINGLE FLAM PARADIDDLE (sometimes called a "Flamadiddle")	 OR 

SOMETHING SPECIAL . . . for drums only

A.

★Check your hand position.

B.

C.

D.

32. WARM-UP

33. READY FOR A NEW NOTE?

NEW NOTE

★ Check the keyboard illustration on page 2-B for the correct bar for G.

34. IN HARMONY

Duet

35. LIP AND TECHNIC BUILDER

★ Write in the counting before you play.

36. TOM DOOLEY AND HIS FRIEND

Folk Song - Duet

37. ODE TO JOY

Ludwig van Beethoven

★ Are you playing with a good hand position?

SOMETHING SPECIAL . . . for mallets only

SPECIAL
EXERCISE

L R L R   L R L R   L   R   R   L   L R L R   R L R L   R   L   R

W3PR - Mallets

| **EIGHTH NOTE** | ♪ = ½ beat

An eighth note is half as long as a quarter note. | 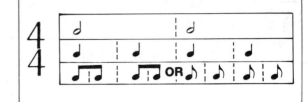 |

38. EIGHTH NOTE COUNTING AND PLAYING

1. Count the rhythm.   2. Write in the counting before you play.

39. CALYPSO SONG

40. CHA CHA RHYTHM

★ Write in the counting before you play.

41. YANKEE DOODLE CHA CHA

42. FEEL THE PULSE

★ Write in the counting before you play.

43. SQUARE DANCE

44. MOVIN' ON UP

★ Write in the counting before you play.

45. THE TALENT SHOW

46. UNEXPECTED EIGHTHS

NEW IDEA

EIGHTH NOTE

 = ½ beat

An eighth note is half as long as a quarter note.

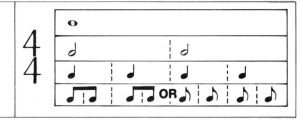

38. EIGHTH NOTE COUNTING AND PLAYING

1. Count the rhythm.   2. Write in the counting before you play.

39. CALYPSO SONG

40. CHA CHA RHYTHM

★ Write in the counting before you play.

41. YANKEE DOODLE CHA CHA

42. FEEL THE PULSE

★ Write in the counting before you play.

43. SQUARE DANCE

44. MOVIN' ON UP

★ Write in the counting before you play.

45. THE TALENT SHOW

46. UNEXPECTED EIGHTHS

47. WARM-UP / 48. TECHNIC BUILDER (B. only)

A. **B.** Play 4 times for the WARM-UP; play 2 times for TECHNIC BUILDER.

49. AURA LEE
Play 4 times.

50. OLD MAC'S FARMYARD

DOTTED HALF NOTE	$2 + 1 = 3$ beats A dot after a note adds half the value of the note.	$\frac{4}{4}$

51. THE DOT MAKES A DIFFERENCE
Play 4 times.

★ Write in the counting for the bass drum part before you play.

52. HELPING HAYDN

1. R R L R R L R R L R R L R R L R R L R R L R L R
2. L R L R L R L R L R L R L R L R L R L R L R L R L

★Draw in the bar lines before you play.

TUTTI **SOLO/SOLI**	Tutti = everyone plays Solo = only one person plays ／ Soli = only one section plays

53. PAW PAW PATCH

Tutti Solo/Soli Tutti

Tutti Solo/Soli Tutti

★Are you playing with a good hand position?

SOMETHING SPECIAL . . . for drums only

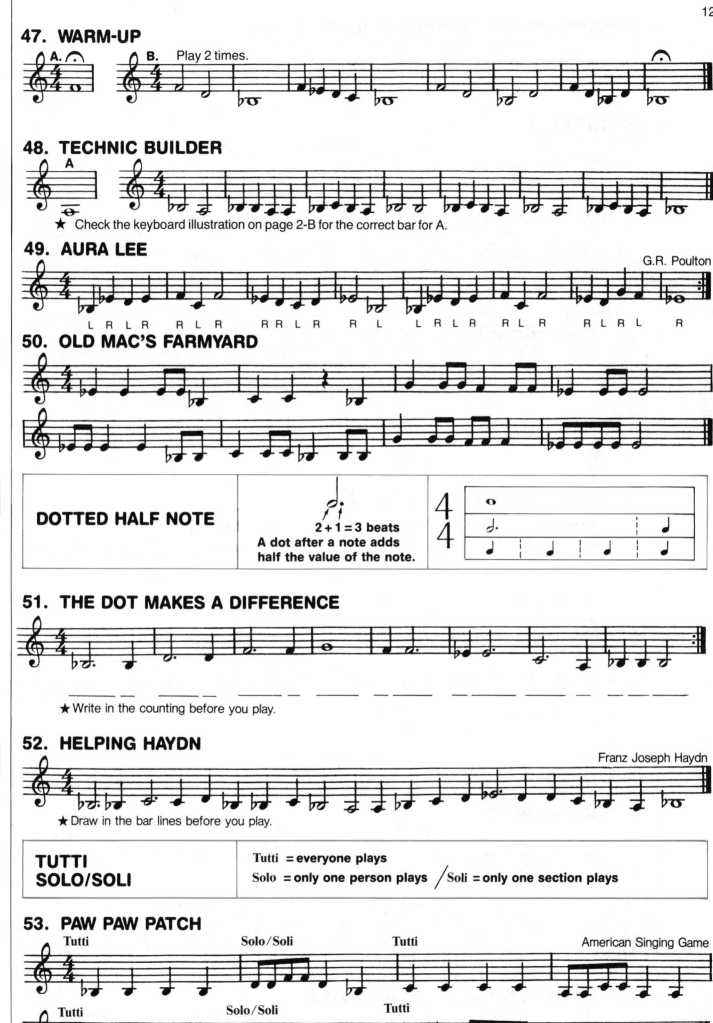

47. WARM-UP

A. **B.** Play 2 times.

48. TECHNIC BUILDER

A

★ Check the keyboard illustration on page 2-B for the correct bar for A.

49. AURA LEE

G.R. Poulton

L R L R   R L R   R R L R   R L   L R L R   R L R   R L R L   R

50. OLD MAC'S FARMYARD

DOTTED HALF NOTE	2 + 1 = 3 beats A dot after a note adds half the value of the note.	$\frac{4}{4}$

51. THE DOT MAKES A DIFFERENCE

★ Write in the counting before you play.

52. HELPING HAYDN

Franz Joseph Haydn

★ Draw in the bar lines before you play.

TUTTI **SOLO/SOLI**	Tutti = everyone plays Solo = only one person plays / Soli = only one section plays

53. PAW PAW PATCH

Tutti   Solo/Soli   Tutti   American Singing Game

Tutti   Solo/Soli   Tutti

★ Are you playing with a good hand position?

NEW NOTE

NEW IDEA

THEORY GAME

NEW IDEA

NEW IDEA

 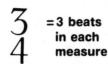 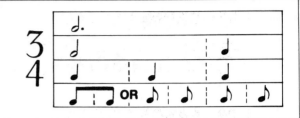

TIME SIGNATURE	$\frac{3}{4}$ = 3 beats in each measure	

54. HEY, DIDDLE DIDDLE / 55. BLOW THE MAN DOWN
Play 2 times for BLOW THE MAN DOWN.

★Write in the counting for the snare drum part before you play.

 NEW IDEA

TIE		A tie is a curved line that connects two notes. Hold the note for the combined value of the two notes.

56. THE TOTAL IS WHAT COUNTS / 57. AUTUMN LEAVES ARE FALLING (Duet)

58. LOVELY EVENING
3-Part Round

SOMETHING SPECIAL . . . for drums only

 SPECIAL EXERCISES

59. RHYTHM PUZZLE

1. Draw in the bar lines. 2. Clap the rhythm before you play.

 THEORY GAME

NEW IDEA

TIME SIGNATURE	$\frac{3}{4}$ = 3 beats in each measure	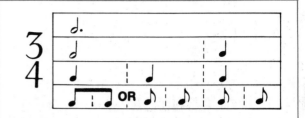

54. HEY, DIDDLE DIDDLE

Traditional

55. BLOW THE MAN DOWN

Traditional Sea Chantey

★ Write in the counting before you play.

NEW IDEA

TIE		A tie is a curved line that connects two notes of the *same* pitch. Hold the note for the combined value of the two notes.

56. THE TOTAL IS WHAT COUNTS

57. AUTUMN LEAVES ARE FALLING

German Folk Song - Duet

58. LOVELY EVENING

3-Part Round

SOMETHING SPECIAL... for mallets only

R L R   L R L   R L R   L R L   R L R   L R L   R L L   R

THEORY GAME

59. RHYTHM PUZZLE

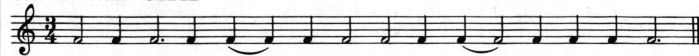

1. Draw in the bar lines.   2. Clap the rhythm before you play.

SPECIAL EXERCISE

60. WARM-UP

61. TONE DEVELOPER / 62. LITTLE CABIN IN THE WOOD

63. THE MAN ON THE FLYING TRAPEZE

64. SMOOTH SOUND

65. SLIPPERY SLURS

66. SPECIAL EFFECTS

★ Do the SPECIAL EFFECTS on mallet page 14-B.

THEORY GAME

NEW IDEA

SPECIAL EXERCISES

| EIGHTH REST | ⁊ = 1/2 beat of silence

An eighth rest is half as long as a quarter rest. | |

SOMETHING SPECIAL . . . for drums only

★ Are you using the correct sticking?

60. WARM-UP

| FLAT | ♭ | | **A flat lowers a note ½ step. It remains in effect for the entire measure.** |

61. TONE DEVELOPER

★ Check the keyboard illustration on page 2-B for the correct bar for A♭.

| KEY SIGNATURE | | **Key signatures change certain notes throughout a piece of music. When you see this key signature, play all B's as B flats, all E's as E flats, and all A's as A flats.** |

62. LITTLE CABIN IN THE WOOD

Traditional

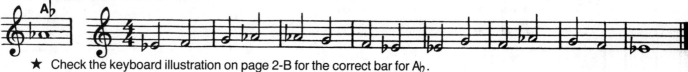

★ Did you check the key signature?

63. THE MAN ON THE FLYING TRAPEZE

George Leybourne

64. SMOOTH SOUND

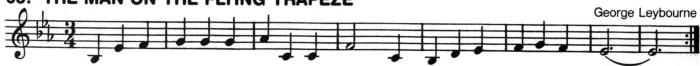

★ Are you striking the bar in the proper place?

65. SLIPPERY SLURS

66. SPECIAL EFFECTS

★ Circle the notes changed by the key signature before you play.

SPECIAL
EXERCISES

NEW
IDEAS

SOMETHING SPECIAL... for drums only

A. READY TO REST

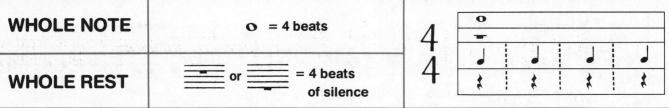

WHOLE NOTE	o = 4 beats	
WHOLE REST	or = 4 beats of silence	

B. TWO LEFT OUT

B.D.

★ Write in the counting for the bass drum part before you play.

C. GRENADIER GUARDS

Solo

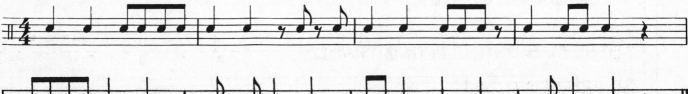

D. HIS MAJESTY

Solo

E. QUARTER AND EIGHTH NOTE REVIEW

★ Write in the counting before you play.

SOMETHING SPECIAL . . . for mallets only

SPECIAL EXERCISES

NEW IDEA

| KEY SIGNATURE | 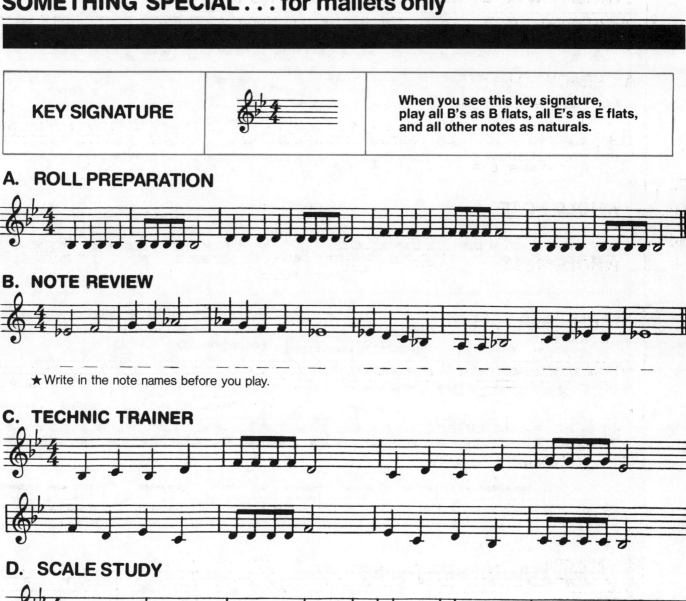 | When you see this key signature, play all B's as B flats, all E's as E flats, and all other notes as naturals. |

A. ROLL PREPARATION

B. NOTE REVIEW

★ Write in the note names before you play.

C. TECHNIC TRAINER

D. SCALE STUDY

L R R L   R L R   L R R L   R L R   R L L R   L R L   L R L R   L R L

E. THIRDS IN MOTION

F. PITCH PLACEMENT

NEW IDEA

| DOUBLE STOPS |  | Play both the upper and lower notes at the same time. |

G. CHORD STUDY

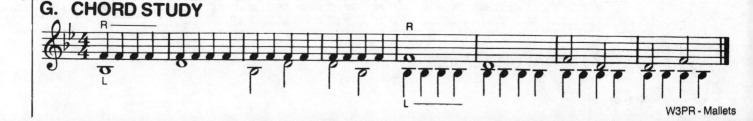

67. WARM-UP

A. **B.** Play 4 times.

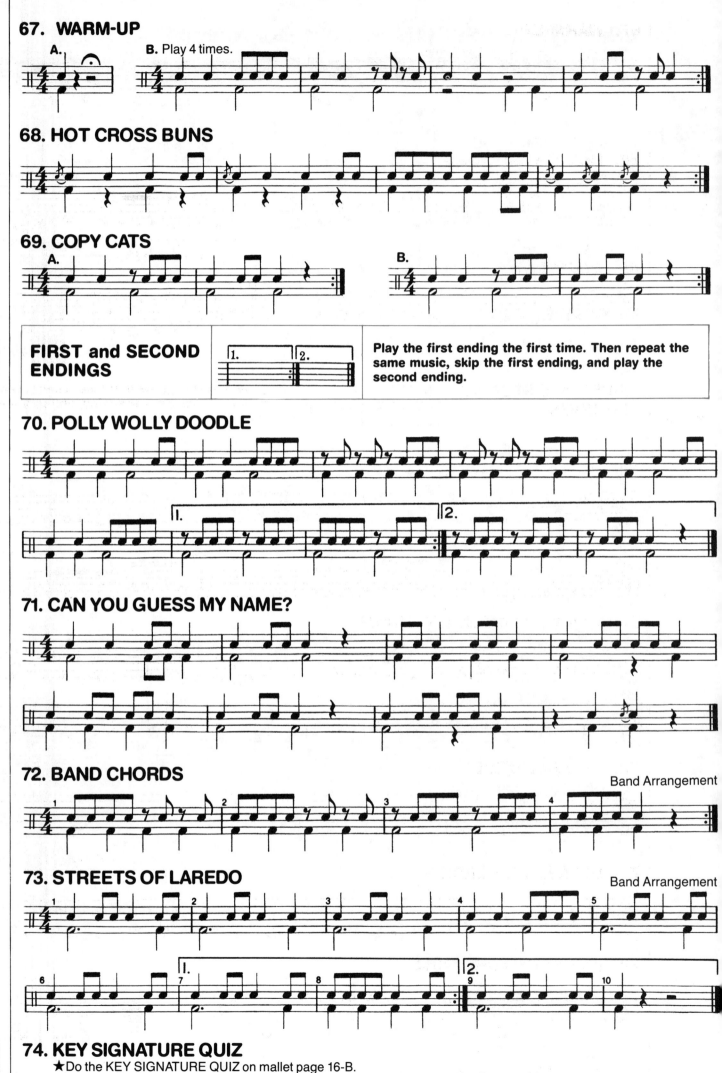

68. HOT CROSS BUNS

69. COPY CATS

A. **B.**

FIRST and SECOND ENDINGS

1. | 2.

Play the first ending the first time. Then repeat the same music, skip the first ending, and play the second ending.

70. POLLY WOLLY DOODLE

1. 2.

71. CAN YOU GUESS MY NAME?

72. BAND CHORDS

Band Arrangement

1 2 3 4

73. STREETS OF LAREDO

Band Arrangement

1 2 3 4 5

1. 2.

6 7 8 9 10

74. KEY SIGNATURE QUIZ

★Do the KEY SIGNATURE QUIZ on mallet page 16-B.

67. WARM-UP

68. HOT CROSS BUNS

English Traditional Song

★ Remember, all A's in this measure are A flats and all B's are B flats.

69. COPY CATS

R L R L   R L R L   R L   R

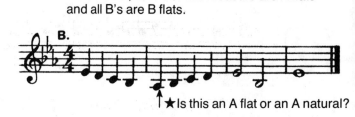

★Is this an A flat or an A natural?

FIRST and SECOND ENDINGS

Play the first ending the first time. Then repeat the same music, skip the first ending, and play the second ending.

NEW IDEA

70. POLLY WOLLY DOODLE

College Song

71. CAN YOU GUESS MY NAME?

72. BAND CHORDS

Band Arrangement

73. STREETS OF LAREDO

Folk Song - Band Arrangement

74. KEY SIGNATURE QUIZ

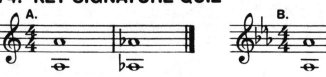

★Write in the note names.

75. WHO WILL PLAY ALL THE RIGHT NOTES?

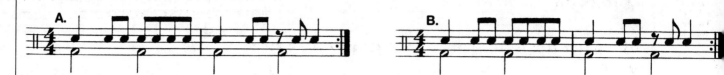

76. WILL YOU GET TRICKED?

| TIME SIGNATURE | $\frac{2}{4}$ = 2 beats in each measure | 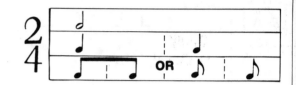 |

77. LITTLE BELLS OF WESTMINSTER

4-Part Round

★Are you playing with a good hand position?

78. THE HARPSICHORD PLAYER

★Write in the counting for the snare drum part before you play.

| D.C. AL FINE | *D.C.* (Da Capo) = beginning
Fine = finish | When you see the *D. C. al Fine*, go back to the beginning and stop when you come to the *Fine*. |
| ABA FORM | | The first musical section A is followed by a new section B. Then section A is repeated. |

79. THE STAR GAZER

80. CONCERTO FOR HAND CLAPPERS, KNEE SLAPPERS, and FOOT STOMPERS

Hand Clappers

Knee Slappers

Foot Stompers

SOMETHING SPECIAL . . . for drums only

NEW IDEA

| NATURAL | ♮ | A natural sign cancels a flat or sharp. It remains in effect for the entire measure. |

75. WHO WILL PLAY ALL THE RIGHT NOTES?

76. WILL YOU GET TRICKED?

NEW IDEA

| TIME SIGNATURE | $\frac{2}{4}$ = 2 beats in each measure | |

77. LITTLE BELLS OF WESTMINSTER

4-Part Round

★Are you playing with a good hand position?

78. THE HARPSICHORD PLAYER

Johann Sebastian Bach

★Write in the counting before you play.

NEW IDEAS

| D.C. AL FINE | D.C. (Da Capo) = beginning
Fine = finish | When you see the D. C. al Fine, go back to the beginning and stop when you come to the Fine. |
| ABA FORM | | The first musical section A is followed by a new section B. Then section A is repeated. |

79. THE STAR GAZER

Folk Melody

Fine

D.C. al Fine

80. CONCERTO FOR HAND CLAPPERS, KNEE SLAPPERS, and FOOT STOMPERS

Hand Clappers

Knee Slappers

Foot Stompers

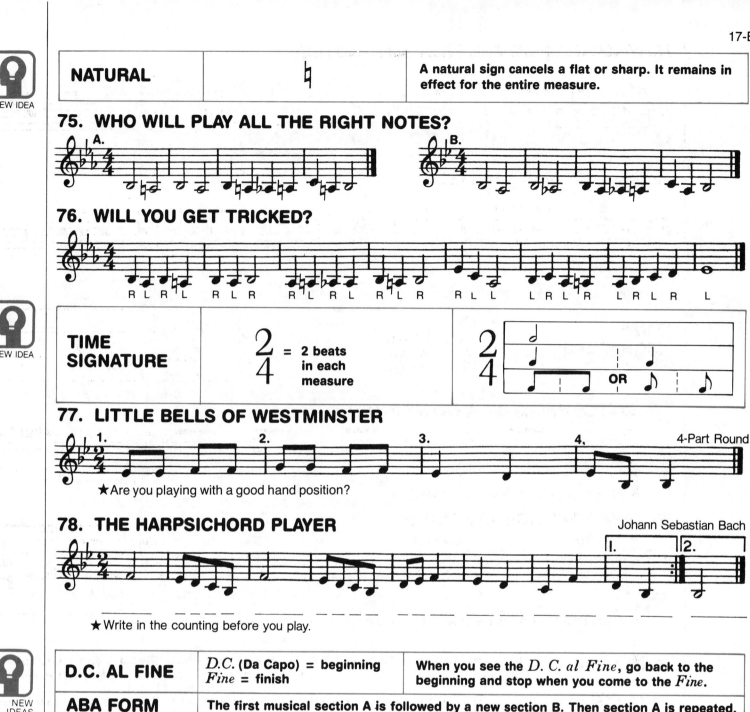

SOMETHING SPECIAL . . . for mallets only

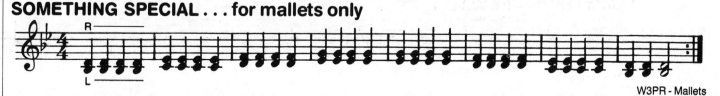

SPECIAL EXERCISE

81. WARM-UP

82. TONE DEVELOPER

83. GO TELL AUNT RHODY

American Folk Song

DOTTED QUARTER NOTE

1 + ½ = 1½ beats

$\frac{2}{4}$

84. TWO WAYS TO PLAY IT

★ Write in the counting before you play.

85. QUARTERBACK SNEAK

R L R L   R L R   R L R L   R   R L R L   R L R   R L R L   R

86. AMERICA

Henry Carey

87. FOLLOW THE LEADER

Solo/Soli   Tutti

Solo/Soli   Tutti

Fine

D. C. al Fine

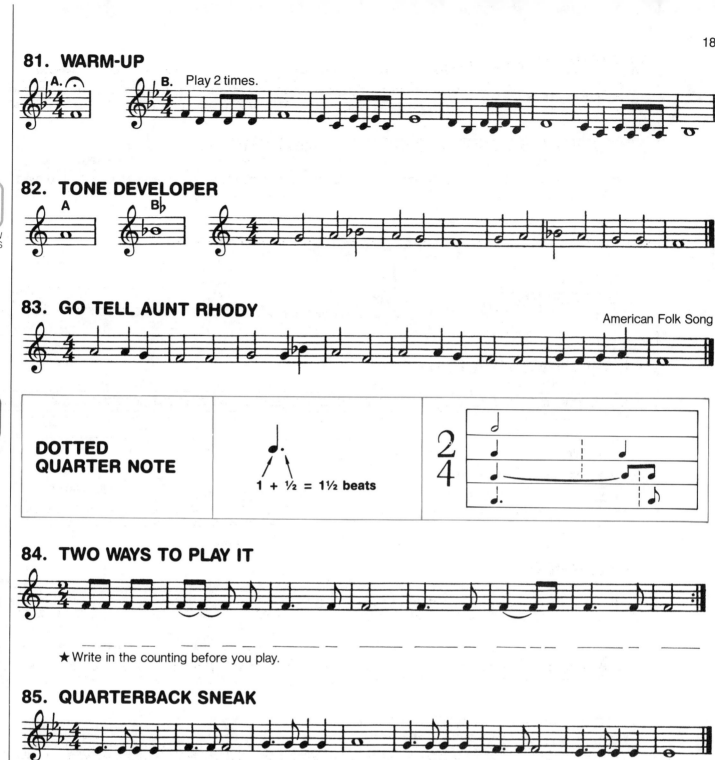

DYNAMICS	f = *forte* p = *piano*	Play with a full volume. Play with a soft volume.
PICK-UP NOTES		Note or notes that come before the first full measure of a piece. (You will first use pick-up notes on page 21.)

WESTERN PORTRAIT

Multiple Percussion Solo

EIGHTH AND SIXTEENTH NOTE COMBINATIONS	$\frac{4}{4}$	

SOMETHING SPECIAL . . . for drums only

Play each measure 4 times.

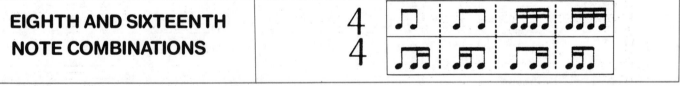

Play each measure 4 times.

Play each measure 4 times.

DYNAMICS	f = *forte* p = *piano*	Play with a full volume. Play with a soft volume.	
PICK-UP NOTES		Note or notes that come before the first full measure of a piece.	

WESTERN PORTRAIT

Root/Pearson

SOMETHING SPECIAL . . . for drums only

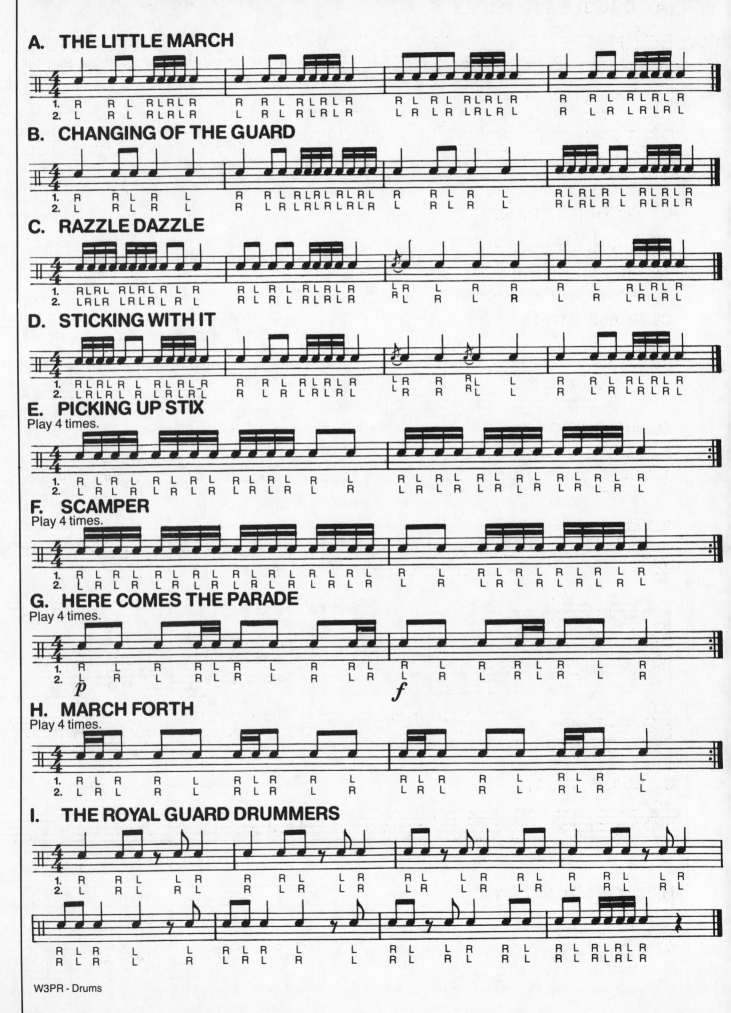

SOMETHING SPECIAL . . . for mallets only

A. DOUBLE STOP DRILL

B. TECHNIC TRAINER

★ Always check the key signature.

C. SCALE STUDY

D. ARPEGGIO STUDY

E. THIRD STUDY

F. ROLL TRAINER

G. SCALE STUDY

★ Did you check the key signature?

H. INTERVAL STUDY

NEW IDEA

REBOUND	WRITTEN	PLAYED	More than one sound with a single stroke. Do not allow the stick to stop on the drum head.
		L L L L R R R R	

88. WARM-UP SCALE / 89. RANGE FINDER / 90. WILL YOU GET CAUGHT?

91. FRERE JACQUES
4-Part Round

92. FOREST GREEN

93. CLARINET CAPERS / 94. MORE CLARINET CAPERS / 95. MUFFINS RISING

96. HOOTCHY KOOTCHY
snares off

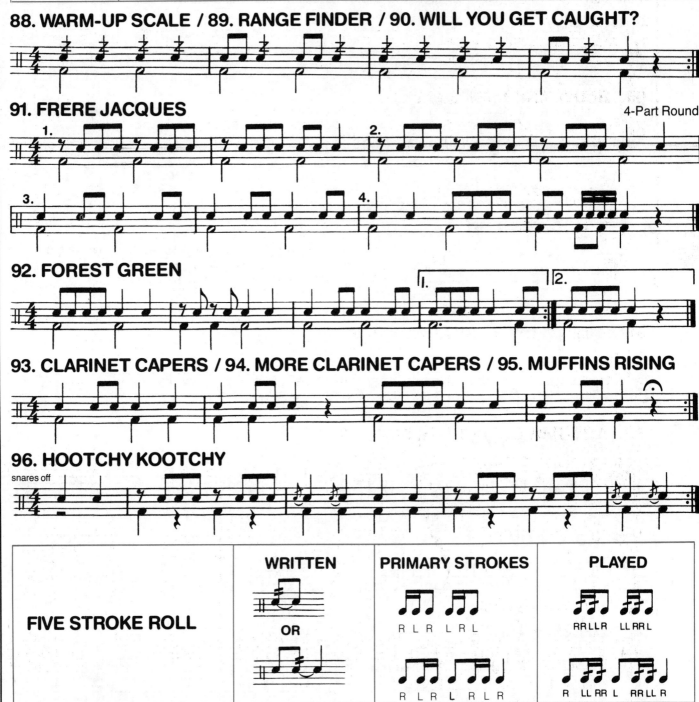

NEW IDEA

FIVE STROKE ROLL	WRITTEN OR	PRIMARY STROKES	PLAYED

SOMETHING SPECIAL . . . for drums only
Play each measure 4 times.
Play each measure 4 times.

SPECIAL EXERCISES

THEORY GAME

97. RHYTHM RAMBLE

1. Draw in the bar lines. 2. Write in the counting before you play.

88. WARM-UP SCALE

★ Is this an A flat or an A natural?

89. RANGE FINDER

90. WILL YOU GET CAUGHT?

91. FRERE JACQUES

4-Part Round

92. FOREST GREEN

Folk Song

93. CLARINET CAPERS

94. MORE CLARINET CAPERS

95. MUFFINS RISING

English Traditional Song

96. HOOTCHY KOOTCHY

Traditional

SOMETHING SPECIAL . . . for mallets only

★ Play smoothly. Play 4 times. Each time you practice, play faster.

97. RHYTHM RAMBLE

1. Draw in the bar lines.   2. Write in the counting before you play.

SPECIAL EXERCISE

THEORY GAME

98. WARM-UP / 99. HOT CROSS BUNS (B. only) / 100. RAINY DAY (B. only)

A. **B.** Play 4 times for the WARM-UP only.

101. PRETZEL PARADE

102. MORNING HAS BROKEN

Play 4 times.

1st time - *f* 2nd time - *p* 3rd time - *f* 4th time - *p*

103. MOLLY MALONE

104. GOING TO THE RACES

Due

NEW IDEA

	WRITTEN	PRIMARY STROKES	PLAYED
NINE STROKE ROLL		R L R L R L R L R L	RR LL RR LL R LL RR LL RR L

SOMETHING SPECIAL . . . for drums only

A. Play 4 times.

1. R L R L R   L   R L R L R   L   R   R   L   R   R   L
2. L R L R L   R   L R L R L   R   L   L   R   L   L   R

B. Play 4 times.

1. R   L   R L R L   L   R L R L   R   L   R   R   L   R L
2. L   R   L R L R   L   L R L R   L   R   L   L   R   L R

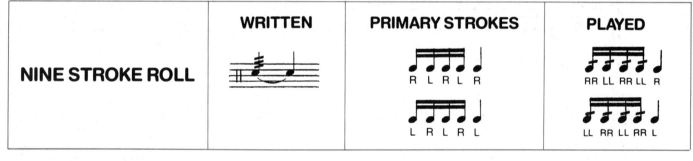

C. Due

SPECIAL
EXERCISES

105. ACCIDENTAL GAME

★ Do the ACCIDENTAL GAME on mallet page 22-B.

THEORY
GAME

98. WARM-UP

99. HOT CROSS BUNS

English Traditional Song

100. RAINY DAY

101. PRETZEL PARADE

102. MORNING HAS BROKEN

Gaelic Melody

103. MOLLY MALONE

Folk Song

104. GOING TO THE RACES

Stephen Foster - Duet

| ROLLS | | Rolls are played by rapidly alternating single strokes. |

SOMETHING SPECIAL . . . for mallets only

L L L R R L L L R R L L L R R L L R R

105. ACCIDENTAL GAME

1. If the second note in each measure is lower than the first note, write **L** for **lower**.
2. If it is the same as the first, write **S** for **same**.
3. If it is higher than the first, write **H** for **higher**.

106. SWEETLY SINGS THE DONKEY / 107. THE DONKEY SINGS IT IN A NEW KEY

2-Part Round

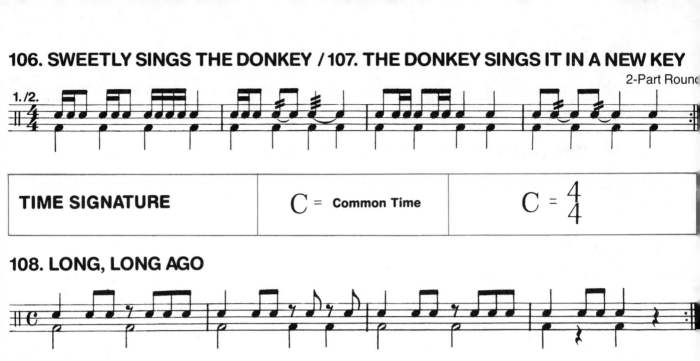

NEW IDEA

TIME SIGNATURE	C = Common Time	C = 4/4

108. LONG, LONG AGO

NEW IDEA

ONE MEASURE REPEAT	𝄎	Repeat the previous measure.

109. FIRST DOWN MARCH

Band Arrangement

110. HERITAGE SONG

111. CHROMATIC MARCH

112. SAME GAME

★Do the SAME GAME on mallet page 23-B.

THEORY
GAME

W3PR - Drums

113. WARM-UP

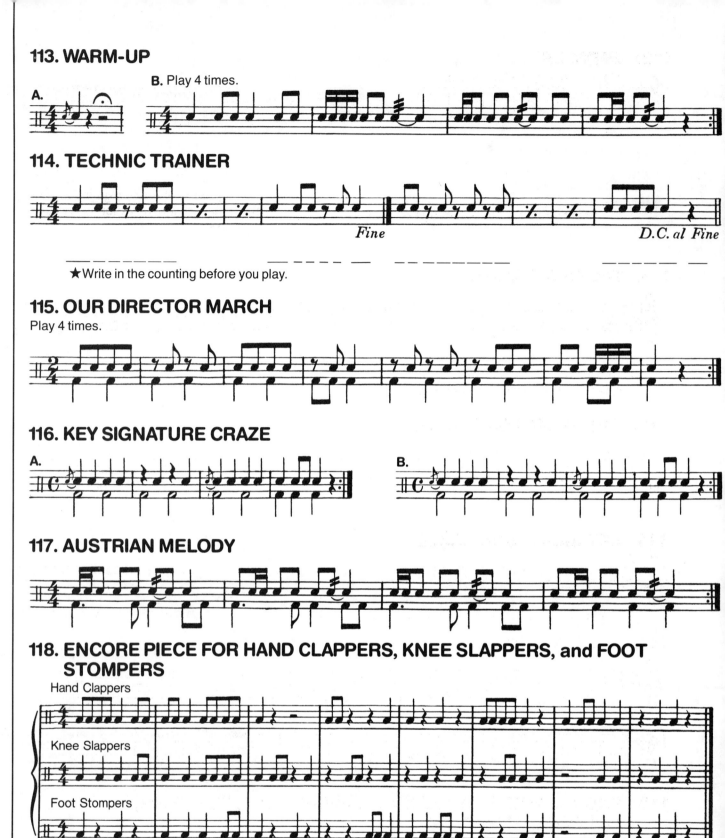

A.

B. Play 4 times.

114. TECHNIC TRAINER

Fine

D.C. al Fine

★Write in the counting before you play.

115. OUR DIRECTOR MARCH

Play 4 times.

116. KEY SIGNATURE CRAZE

A.

B.

117. AUSTRIAN MELODY

118. ENCORE PIECE FOR HAND CLAPPERS, KNEE SLAPPERS, and FOOT STOMPERS

Hand Clappers

Knee Slappers

Foot Stompers

SOMETHING SPECIAL . . . for drums only

SPECIAL
EXERCISES

A.

1. R L R   R L R   R L R   R R R   R R L R   R L R L R   R   R   R L R R   R
2. L R L   R L R L   L R L   R R L   L R L   R L R L R L R L R   R   R L R L R R L

B.

1. R L R L R   R   R L R L   R R   R L R R   R R R   R L R L R   R L R L R   R   R   R
2. L R L R L   R L R L R   L R R L R L L   R L R L R   L R L R L   R   R   L   L

C.

1. R L R L R   R L R   R   R L R   R L R L R L R L   R L R L R   R L R L R   R L R L R
2. L R L R L   R L R   L   L   R L R   L R L R L R L R L R   R L R L R   R   R

113. WARM-UP

| KEY SIGNATURE |  | When you see this key signature, play all B's as B flats and all other notes as naturals. |

114. TECHNIC TRAINER

★ Write in the counting before you play.

115. OUR DIRECTOR MARCH

F.E. Bigelow

116. KEY SIGNATURE CRAZE

117. AUSTRIAN MELODY

Franz Joseph Haydn

118. ENCORE PIECE FOR HAND CLAPPERS, KNEE SLAPPERS, and FOOT STOMPERS

SOMETHING SPECIAL . . . for mallets only

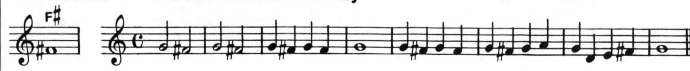

119. SERENADE

1st time - *f* ★ Did you play the *forte* full and the *piano* soft?
2nd time - *p*

120. SIMPLE GIFTS / 121. SUNTAN SERENADE (Duet)

★ Play with dynamics for SIMPLE GIFTS; play without dynamics for SUNTAN SERENADE.

122. THIS OLD MAN HAS RHYTHM

★ Write in the counting before you play.

123. TIJUANA TILLY'S

Band Arrangement

Cowbell

★ In ¾ time a whole rest equals a whole measure (3 beats).

	WRITTEN	PRIMARY STROKES	PLAYED
SEVENTEEN STROKE ROLL		R L R L R L R L R L R L R L R L R L	R R L L R R L L R R L L R R L L R L L R R L L R R L L R R L L R R L

NEW IDEA

SOMETHING SPECIAL . . . for drums only

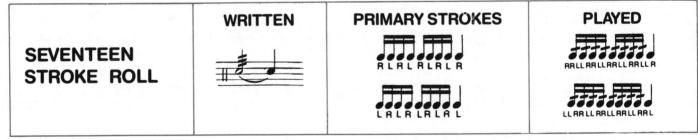

A.
1. R L R L R L R L R — R — R — R L R L R L R L R — R — R —
2. L R L R L R L R L — L — L — L R L R L R L R L — L — L —

SPECIAL EXERCISES

B.
1. R — R L — R L R L R L R L — R — R L R — R — R L R L R L R L R — R — R
2. L — R L — R L R L R L R L — R — L R L — R L R L R L R L — L — R — R

124. ACCIDENTAL GAME

★ Do the ACCIDENTAL GAME on mallet page 25-B.

THEORY GAME

119. SERENADE

Johann Sebastian Bach

★ Did you play the *forte* full and the *piano* soft?

120. SIMPLE GIFTS

Shaker Song

★ Are you playing with a good hand position?

121. SUNTAN SERENADE

Root - Duet

A.

B.

122. THIS OLD MAN HAS RHYTHM

★ Write in the counting before you play.

123. TIJUANA TILLY'S

Root/Pearson - Band Arrangement

★ In ¾ time a whole rest equals a whole measure (3 beats).

SOMETHING SPECIAL . . . for mallets only

124. ACCIDENTAL GAME

1. If the second note in each measure is lower than the first note, write **L** for **lower**.
2. If it is the same as the first, write **S** for **same**.
3. If it is higher than the first, write **H** for **higher**.

W3PR - Mallets

SOMETHING SPECIAL . . . for drums only

A. 17 STROKE SALUTE

B. STRUTTIN' SEVENTEENS

C. SIMPLY SEVENTEEN

D. FABULOUS FIVES

E. NOTHING BUT NINES

F. RAMBLIN' ROLLS

G. WHERE'S THE BEAT?

W3PR - Drums

SOMETHING SPECIAL . . . for mallets only

A. SCALE STUDY

B. SHORTNIN' BREAD

Traditional

C. LET'S BOOGIE

★Play all E's as E naturals.

D. GETTING THERE

E. GOING SOMEWHERE

F. ARPEGGIO STUDY

G. DOUBLE JOY

Ludwig van Beethoven

125. A CHROMATIC VIEW POINT

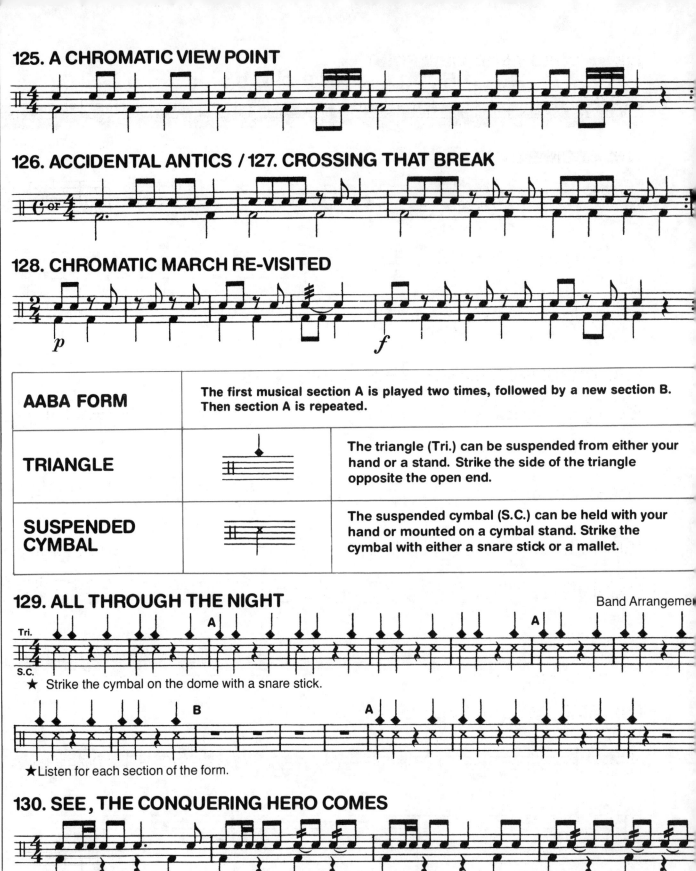

126. ACCIDENTAL ANTICS / 127. CROSSING THAT BREAK

128. CHROMATIC MARCH RE-VISITED

AABA FORM		The first musical section A is played two times, followed by a new section B. Then section A is repeated.
TRIANGLE		The triangle (Tri.) can be suspended from either your hand or a stand. Strike the side of the triangle opposite the open end.
SUSPENDED CYMBAL		The suspended cymbal (S.C.) can be held with your hand or mounted on a cymbal stand. Strike the cymbal with either a snare stick or a mallet.

129. ALL THROUGH THE NIGHT

Band Arrangement

Tri.

S.C.

★ Strike the cymbal on the dome with a snare stick.

★ Listen for each section of the form.

130. SEE, THE CONQUERING HERO COMES

131. FOLLOW THE LEADER

Solo/Soli   Tutti

132. NAME GAME

★ Do the NAME GAME on mallet page 27-B.

NEW IDEAS

THEORY GAME

125. A CHROMATIC VIEW POINT

L R L R R L R R L R R L R L L R L R R L R L L R L R R R

126. ACCIDENTAL ANTICS

★ Remember the key signature.

127. CROSSING THAT BREAK

128. CHROMATIC MARCH RE-VISITED

AABA FORM	The first musical section A is played two times, followed by a new section B. Then section A is repeated.

129. ALL THROUGH THE NIGHT

Old Welsh Song - Band Arrangement

★ Listen for each section of the form.

130. SEE, THE CONQUERING HERO COMES

George Frideric Handel

131. FOLLOW THE LEADER

132. NAME GAME

★ Write in the note names and their accidentals.

NEW
IDEAS

DYNAMICS	= *crescendo* (*cresc.*)	**Gradually play louder.**
	= *decrescendo* (*decresc.*)	**Gradually play softer.**
ACCENT		**Play the note with the accent (>) a little louder.**

133. WARM-UP

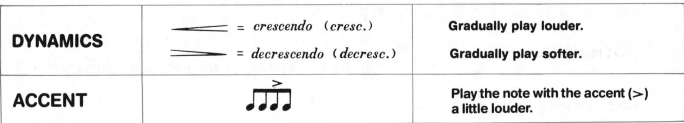

134. BOOGIE BEAT

135. CHROMATIC WALTZ

136. THE MINSTREL BOY

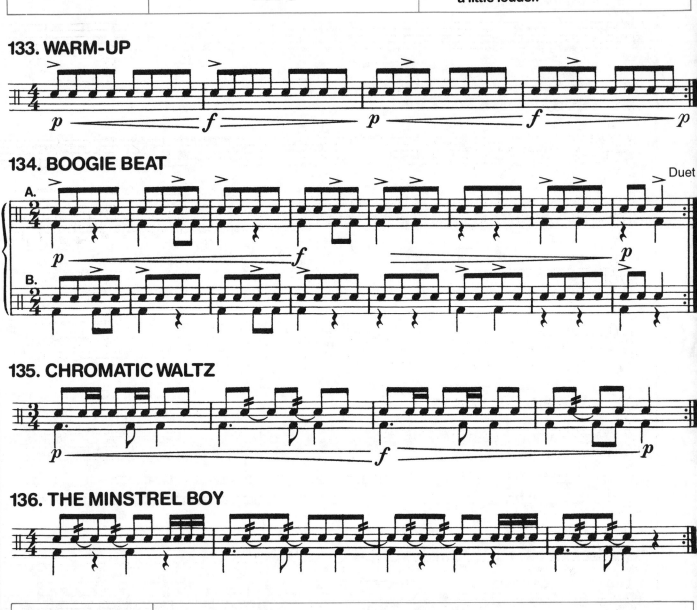

NEW IDEA

THEME AND VARIATIONS	A simple tune followed by the same tune with changes.

137. WHERE DID MY LITTLE DOG GO?

Theme

Variation

SOMETHING SPECIAL . . . for drums only
Play each exercise 4 times.

SPECIAL
EXERCISES

| DYNAMICS | = crescendo (cresc.) | Gradually play louder. |
| | = decrescendo (decresc.) | Gradually play softer. |

THEME AND VARIATIONS — A simple tune followed by the same tune with changes.

137. WHERE DID MY LITTLE DOG GO?

SOMETHING SPECIAL... for mallets only

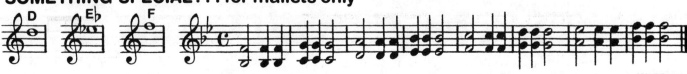

NEW IDEA

| DYNAMICS | *mp* = *mezzo piano* | Play with a medium soft volume. |
| | *mf* = *mezzo forte* | Play with a medium full volume. |

138. SCARBOROUGH FAIR

139. POLISHED PHRASES

Band Arrangement

NEW IDEA

TEMPOS	Andante = moderately slow
	Moderato = moderate speed
	Allegro = quick and lively

140. BRING A TORCH

Moderato

141. BAYSIDE BOUNCE

Allegro

Band Arrangement

Cowbell

142. CHROMATIC CAPER

Andante   Play 4 times.

143. PUTTING IT ALL TOGETHER

W3PR - Drums

NEW IDEA

| DYNAMICS | *mp* = *mezzo piano* | Play with a medium soft volume. |
| | *mf* = *mezzo forte* | Play with a medium full volume. |

138. SCARBOROUGH FAIR

English Folk Song

NEW IDEA

| PHRASE | A musical thought or sentence. |

139. POLISHED PHRASES

Root - Band Arrangement

NEW IDEA

TEMPOS	Andante = moderately slow
	Moderato = moderate speed
	Allegro = quick and lively

140. BRING A TORCH

French Song

Moderato

★ Check your hand position.

141. BAYSIDE BOUNCE

Root/Pearson -Band Arrangement

Allegro

142. CHROMATIC CAPER

Andante

mf

143. PUTTING IT ALL TOGETHER

L R L R L R L R   L R L R L   L R L R L R L R   L R L R L

R L R L R L R L   R L R L R   R L R L R L R L   R L R L R

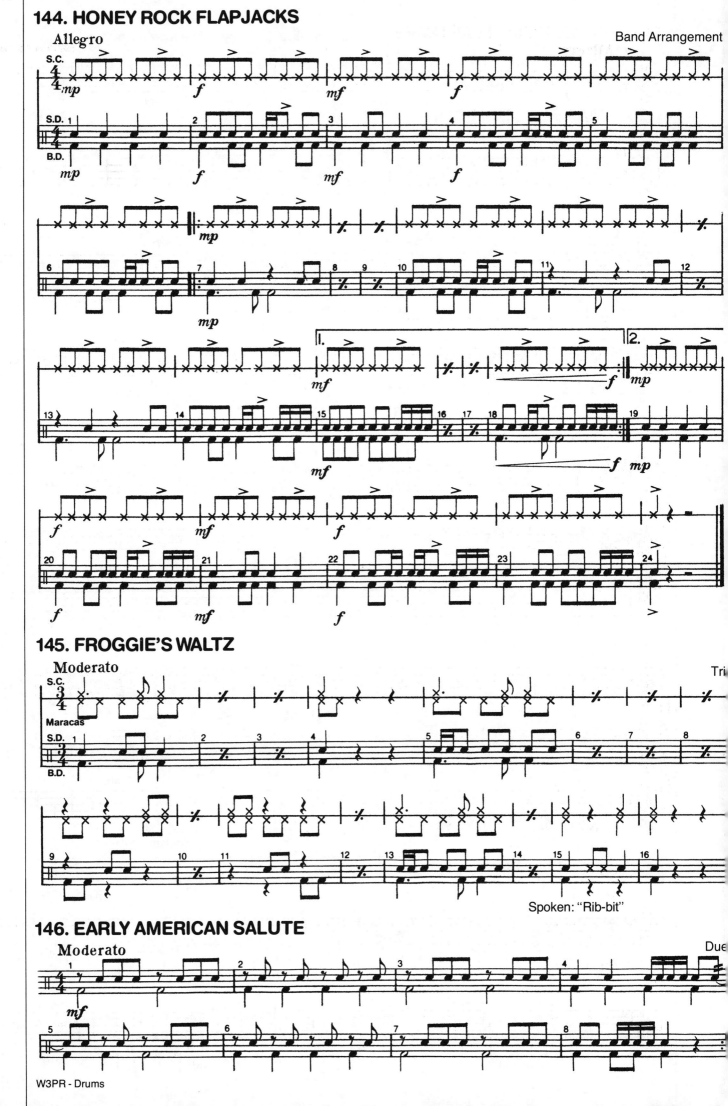

144. HONEY ROCK FLAPJACKS

Band Arrangement

145. FROGGIE'S WALTZ

Spoken: "Rib-bit"

146. EARLY AMERICAN SALUTE

144. HONEY ROCK FLAPJACKS

Band Arrangement

145. FROGGIE'S WALTZ

Root/Pearson - Trio

Spoken: "Rib-bit"

146. EARLY AMERICAN SALUTE

Billings/Pearson-Duet

147. JINGLE BELLS

148. COWBOYS AND CACTUS

149. BUMPY ROAD

W3PR - Drums

147. JINGLE BELLS

Pierpont/Pearson - Band Arrangement

148. COWBOYS AND CACTUS

Root/Pearson - Band Arrangement

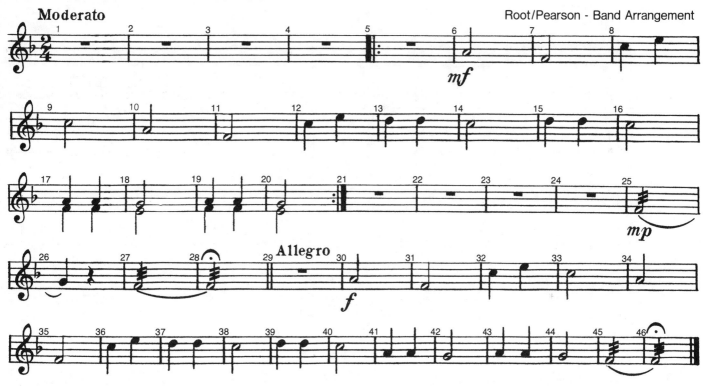

149. BUMPY ROAD

Band Arrangement

IT'S ALL YOURS!

This special page of pieces is for extra practice and fun on your instrument.
The pieces may be played with the mallet part on page 32-B to make percussion
ensembles. They may also be used as an accompaniment to any other solo
instrument playing this page.

IT'S ALL YOURS!

This special page of solos is for extra practice and fun on your instrument.
The pieces may be played by themselves or along with the piano part found
in the piano accompaniment book.

JINGLE BELLS

J.S. Pierpont

GOOD KING WENCESLAS

English Carol

HOLIDAY GREETINGS

English Carol

GO, TEAM, GO!

Go, Team, Go!

SAINTS GO MARCHING IN

Traditional

AMERICA

Henry Carey

W3PR - Mallets

GLOSSARY

Term	Symbol	Definition

RHYTHM—Notes and Rests

	Notes	Rests	
WHOLE	o	▬	4 beats
DOTTED HALF	𝅗𝅥.		3 beats
HALF	𝅗𝅥	▬	2 beats
DOTTED QUARTER	♩.		1½ beats
QUARTER	♩	𝄽	1 beat
EIGHTH	♪	𝄾	½ beat
SIXTEENTH	𝅘𝅥𝅯		¼ beat

RHYTHM—Time Signatures

Term	Symbol	Definition
FOUR-FOUR TIME	$\frac{4}{4}$	4 beats in each measure
COMMON TIME	C	4 beats in each measure (same as $\frac{4}{4}$)
THREE-FOUR TIME	$\frac{3}{4}$	3 beats in each measure
TWO-FOUR TIME	$\frac{2}{4}$	2 beats in each measure

BASICS

Term	Symbol	Definition
STAFF		
LEDGER LINE		used to extend the staff
TREBLE CLEF		
FLAT	♭	lowers a note ½ step
SHARP	♯	raises a note ½ step
NATURAL	♮	cancels a flat or sharp
KEY SIGNATURES		flats or sharps at the beginning of a piece that change certain notes throughout the piece
PICK-UP NOTES		note or notes that come before the first full measure of a piece
REPEAT SIGN		play the previous section of music again
ONE MEASURE REPEAT		repeat the previous measure